Laurel Tu

M000028670

Distracted Driving... crosses the line

By Vincent Carbone

All rights reserved. This book is protected by the copyright laws of the United States of America. This book may not be copied or reprinted for commercial gain or profit. The use of short quotations or occasional page copying for personal or group study is permitted and encouraged. Permission will be granted upon request.
Unless otherwise identified, all Scripture quotations are from the New International Version. Copyright © 2011 by Zondervan, Inc. Used by permission. All rights reserved. The following books were used by permission: Taken from: *Sitting at the Feet of Rabbi Jesus*, by Ann Spangler and Lois Tverberg, Copyright © by Ann Spangler and Lois Tverberg. Used by permission of Zondervan.
Taken from: *Walking in the Dust of Rabbi Jesus*, by Lois Tverberg, Copyright © 2012 by Lois Tverberg. Used by permission of Zondervan.

For Worldwide Distribution, Printed in the U.S.A.

ISBN: 978-0-692-03589-4

Distracted Driving...crosses the line
By Vincent Carbone
Printed by Kindle Direct Publishing
Copyright 2018
Cover Design by **Gallagher Media, Inc.**

DEDICATION

To Beth

I am fortunate to be married to my best friend.

To Vinny, Julie, Breanne and Jimmy

I am happy to still be a part of your lives.
You are all amazing.

CONTENTS

ACKNOWLEDGMENTS

Thank you

On behalf of the entire Carbone family, I want to express our love and deep gratitude to many people. Words do not capture how our hearts feel towards each of you.

I want to thank David Wagner who prophesized and prayed over me while I was in ICU that first week of the crash. He prayed that I would one day write a book and travel and minister with him once again. Now that the book is complete, I look forward to ministering with him in the near future.

I want to thank the entire Monroe Volunteer Fire, and Monroe Volunteer EMS Departments for responding quickly and with great care. I want to thank David York for holding bags of plasma up to keep me alive and for EMS worker Tim for finding my glasses in the back seat.

I want to thank the incredible staff at St. Vincent's Hospital in Bridgeport, CT and Gaylord Specialty Healthcare in Wallingford, CT.

I want to thank Dr. Dante Brittis of Orthopaedic Specialty Group for keeping me alive that first night. Thank you, Dr. Rolf Langeland of Orthopaedic Specialty Group, who is now part of Lifespan and Newport Orthopedics of Newport, Rhode Island. As far as I know, I still hold the record for the most surgeries performed by him. Yeah!

Thank you, Brian Christy, my old physical therapist, for working out with me at his friend's gym on his free days. I really appreciate how he took the time and effort to develop a program for me on his own initiative.

I want to thank the entire staff of IMed Chiropractic of Fairfield for their great ongoing care.

I want to thank my family of colleagues at Fairfield Woods Middle School, the Woods community and for the town of Fairfield for their incredible support and love. Thank you, Ann Leffert for all your help and support. Thank you, Bea Bagley and Margaret Richter for being such great teammates. I worked with Bea for about twenty-five years in the elementary and middle school. Bea asked me to follow her to the middle school, and I am so thankful to her for encouraging me to make that move. I am just saddened that I was absent for her last few years before her retirement. Team teaching with Bea, has been the highlight of my career.

Thank you, Masuk High School and the many Monroe families that gathered around my family with so much support and love.

Thank you, Ai Lin Lim and De Wen Soh for your incredible support and encouragement. Thank you to our entire Valley Shore Church family.

Thank you to my good friend and incredible artist Joy Gallagher for helping me with the book title and for creating the book cover. Thank you, Jim Gallagher for editing the transcript.

Thank you, Trace Evans for helping me with the publishing process. While I will be mentioning more individuals in the book, I want to thank two great friends Ted Josephson and Mark Behm who are each closer to me than a brother.

Beth and I visiting the Monroe Volunteer Fire Department and Monroe Volunteer EMS. We visited them sometime in September 2015 to thank them. Tim is standing next to me. He located my glasses in the car.

David York is the older man in the center of the picture. They all wanted to know what kind of car it was, because they could not identify it. These individuals are real heroes.

Author's Note

I honor Candace Lightner's incredible leadership. Her efforts helped shift an entire mindset and attitude in our culture in one generation concerning drinking and driving. It is truly an amazing task. Rarely does anyone have that kind of influence. She fought against the prevailing mindset and attitude in the day and time that said, "Boys will be boys", concerning alcohol and driving. Her work transformed the way we think about people being held responsible for their actions. She founded two organizations, M.A.D.D. Mothers Against Drunk Driving and We Save Lives. Her leadership led to the passage of more than 500 bills at the state and national levels and for establishing the minimum age for drinking at 21. Her efforts have influenced the safety of our roads for generations. While it has been 38 years since her precious daughter Cari was killed by a drunk driver, her pain is still fresh. Her pain continues to fuel her efforts so others do not have to endure similar pain.

It is hard to conceive that people are still being arrested today for driving under the influence of alcohol with our strict laws. This speaks more to the power of addiction. It is time for another mindset shift concerning distracted driving, and texting in particular. Distracted driving is just as disabling as a person driving under the influence of alcohol, and just as addicting. The only difference is that texting and driving is generally accepted in our society. The scary reality is that more people are distracted while driving than driving under the influence of alcohol.

"Do you know what you just did?" asked Jody Kuchler to twenty-year-old Jack Dillion Young. "I'm sorry, I'm sorry. I was texting." While Young was later charged for being intoxicated, these were Young's first words after his pickup truck collided head-on with a church van killing 13 people in Uvalde, Texas, on March 29, 2017. The unfortunate part was that Jody Kuchler was pleading with a 911 dispatcher to get someone to come and address the erratic driver before it was too late. Kuchler followed Young's pick-up truck for 14 minutes. In the NTSB report, Young's pickup crossed the yellow line 19 times and the white shoulder line 37 times prior to the crash. The officials were too late in sending help to the scene. Jody Kuchler should not have had to plead with the 911 dispatcher to send help.

Too many innocent people have been killed or have suffered some physical disability due to distracted driving. This author is pleading with young people and older people to understand the great responsibility they take when getting behind the wheel of a vehicle. He also pleads with legislatures to make stiffer penalties. Paying a $150 fine might not change future driving attitudes and behaviors with regards to distracted driving. Instead, I believe that distracted drivers' license should be taken away for a brief period of time- even a few months. Penalties like this might have a greater impact to changing drivers' attitudes with regards to texting. I plead with law enforcement to think up creative ways to enforce these laws. Distracted driving crosses the line and we need to end it in this generation. Can one imagine finding out that injuries resulted from a distracted pilot, distracted air traffic controller, distracted surgeon or any profession where people's lives are at stake? There is zero tolerance for distractions in professions dealing with people. Why, then, do we accept distracted drivers where millions of people are at risk every day?

I will provide an URL page so that health teachers, driving school instructors and others can download my PowerPoint to use with their students. Please read my story and realize that these consequences were totally avoidable. If laws and the enforcement of laws are not revised nor followed, these consequences have a good chance of one day impacting your family. Continuing to text and drive is like playing Russian roulette with a fully loaded gun. Make a commitment today to drive mindfully.

URL: https://drive.google.com/drive/u/0/my-drive
Distracted Driving...crosses the line

This is the Carbone family before a head-on crash involving My wife and me. Jimmy, Vinny, Beth, me with Hershey, Breanne and Julie.

1 Introduction

My mind was elsewhere. I was preoccupied with going back to work on Monday. It was a sunny, warm Friday afternoon and the end of our April school break. I was tired because I had spent the last three days going in and out of New York with my kids. My triplet children were graduating in a little over a month and I wanted to spend some quality time with them. I went to the art museum with Julie on Tuesday, Little Italy and Times Square with Breanne on Wednesday, and I spent a late night at City Field Thursday with Jimmy. My wife and I were driving home from my son Jimmy's volleyball game. He had driven himself to the game and was still cleaning up when we left. I was thinking about being home and relaxing. We were only two miles from home on route 111. The road is a two-lane road that winds through rural Monroe into its business area. The drive home was quiet.

I was going through the motions as if I was on automatic. The car knew the route. I drove this way hundreds of times.

Then I saw it. It jolted me back to reality. The white SUV registered confusion at first. Wasted seconds. The vehicle came around the corner and shook sideways as the driver straightened it out. Two things came to my mind. That vehicle was moving too fast and it was in my lane. Confusion. Why was this vehicle in my lane coming straight at me? More wasted time. I yelled, "Why aren't they moving over?" There were no cars in the other lane. I had nowhere to go, because guardrails lined this part of the road. I could not go to the other lane. I was convinced the SUV was going to go back. Was this actually happening?

I was part of the blast. My small car. The SUV. They were one. And I was somehow one with it all. A fireball. Glass. Metal. White. An intense white. Roar and reverberation. Glass flew outwards and at me screaming. Shrieking slivers of glass filled the air around my head. Flying past me with great speed, glass continued to explode apart. Metal stretched and detonated with a screeching thunderclap that went through me. An intense white roared around me. It filled my eyes, my ears, my mouth, my head. The scream. A death scream came from deep within. As quickly as it came, it was over. But not my scream. Beth grabbed me as she turned on the light.

My scream quickly turned to crying. I was crying uncontrollably." You're fine. You're fine. Everything is okay." Beth reassured me. I was in the safety of my bedroom, but not in my heart and definitely not my mind. I was there once again. It was real. So scary real. Am I losing my mind? I could not go back to sleep. I could not close my eyes. I did not want to go back 'there'. The bathroom door was left ajar so light could spill into my room. Beth tried to go back to sleep, but I couldn't.

A few nights earlier I had experienced a similar nightmare. I flung my feet and legs out trying to free myself. I was trapped in the car and I could not get out. I was pinned in. Deep heavy breaths. Trapped. Hot. Suffocating. Dark. Not knowing where up and down were. The covers lifted off me as I continued to kick off anything holding me down. It took a lot of time for my heart to stop racing and for my wife's soothing voice to bring me back to reality. Light. Fresh air. Safety.

Distracted driving: An Emerging Epidemic

We need to raise the seriousness of the consequences for distracted driving, to mirror the consequences of DUI penalties. Here is a chilling thought about the addictive nature of these devices. In October 2015 CNN published an article about 13-year-olds: The article reported that some 13-year-olds check social media 100 times a day. The following are two quotes:

"I would rather not eat for a week than get my phone taken away."[1]

"It's really bad," said Gia, a 13-year-old. "I literally feel like I'm going to die."[2]

In three short years those young people will be driving our roads. Changes need to be made today that will ensure those roads are safe for them, and you. "Five seconds is the average time your eyes are off the road while texting. When traveling at 55 mph, that's enough time to cover the length of a football field blindfolded. At any given daylight moment across America, approximately 660,000 drivers are using cell phones or manipulating electronic devices while driving. That number has held steady since 2010. After steady declines over the last four decades, highway fatalities last year recorded the largest annual percentage increase in 50 years.[3]

It never entered my mind that a person would drive a vehicle and have their eyes and mind elsewhere because of their phone and its many tempting apps. I thought the driver who hit me was contemplating a steering correction while in my lane. In my opinion, she never saw me. She was **intexticated**. It was established in the police report that the other driver was on Snapchat for at least three minutes before the crash. This is where I have to clearly state that it is in my opinion that she was distracted because of her phone. If not, my lawyer has advised me that she could bring a legal suit against me. Can you begin to identify with my anger? It seemed so ironic that this person who destroyed my body, almost took the lives of myself and my wife, and turned my car into a crushed tin can could possibly sue me for a simple statement I make. How is it that the law could protect her name while ignore my need for justice? I learned through this experience that many of our current laws have many flaws. I have so much to say about this later.

My high school graduation picture had this quote from the Bible underneath my picture. Proverbs 3:5-6 (NIV) "Trust in the LORD with all your heart and lean not on your own understanding; in all your ways submit to him, and he will make your paths straight." Little did I know that an SUV would one day be in my path. How do I reconcile what happened to me and my family? Where was God in the midst of my experience of injustice, anger, and confusion? It wasn't just one act of injustice.

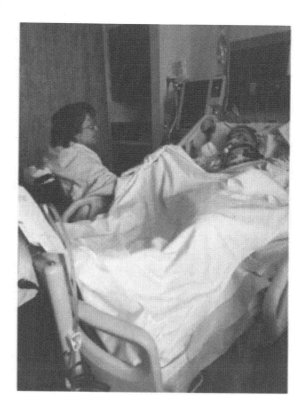

Two Hearts

Two hearts skipped a beat.
And in that second, they were fighting for their lives
To change the tragedy that was coming their way.
Trapped.
Silence disturbed by sirens.
As they tore apart what was left, two loving souls held on.
Adrenaline rushed through their bodies like electricity.
Hearts of a fighter.
Brave, kind hearted, loving.
The two hearts found their way back to one another.
The warmth of their hands kept them connected.
They looked at one another with such passion and grace.
When his heart began to yearn for hers, she felt his pain.
Weeping together in silence.
Letting their bodies relieve the pain.

By Julie Carbone

2 THE CRASH

Julie had made a last-minute decision not to come to Jimmy's volleyball game. I stood in the driveway deciding which vehicle to take. The van was low on gas, so I took the PT Cruiser. I had only had it for a few months and I hated it. It maneuvered terribly. The horn was something I would find on my old Schwinn bike. It was embarrassing. No one responds or even hears it. It was small. It had horrible vision out the back. It felt like a death trap. There seemed to have very little protection, because it was a small car. I would never buy such a car. But, it had been free.

I had three children ready to graduate from high school. My oldest son was in his first year of school overseas. We had to put down our much-loved dog, Hershey, because the bills were now going to reach thousands of dollars and nothing was helping him. He was old and I had four children and their education to worry about. He fought it long enough and late into November 2014. We had to put him down. It was one of the hardest things to do. We all mourned into 2015.

I purchased a car in 2013 and it died in December of 2014. My mother offered the PT Cruiser for me to keep. She did not need two cars now that my step-dad was no longer able to drive. I was not to go in debt when I had a perfectly good car. I could put up with it for now.

My wife and I took the car to the game at Masuk High School. I took some pictures on my phone. We headed home. Beth's brother, Kevin, was visiting his father who was ninety-one and having some health issues. He was at Bridgeport Hospital. Beth's mom was home nursing a broken ankle. It was Friday, April 17, 2015. It was a beautiful sunny but warm day. I had my window down. I was emotionally exhausted. It was the end of spring vacation. I had taken Jimmy to City Field the night before to watch the Mets and Marlins. Wednesday, I had taken Breanne to Little Italy in New York. We spent the day walking all over Manhattan. Tuesday, I had taken Julie to the Met to look at the great artists. The only person I had not done anything for that week was Beth. I was also going through some difficult issues at school. I was tired. I was entering the perfect storm. I had to make a quick decision and I was on empty.

The white SUV rocked back and forth as it turned the corner and it was fully in my lane. This vehicle was moving. It rocked from side to side as it maneuvered the curve. I was confused at first. Why are they in my lane? There was no one else in their lane. "Why aren't they moving back over?" I screamed it now. "They are going to move over! Right?" It was like a fastball coming at my head. I had nowhere to go. There was no shoulder on my right, only a guardrail. My two hands gripped the wheel. I couldn't go in the other lane. They are going back over. I will hit them and it will be my fault. I thought all of this and then it was too late. The surreal was actually happening.

The front-end view of my car resting at the junkyard.

The first thing I noticed during the crash was this electric buzz going through my body starting from my feet to my head. It didn't hurt at all. I opened my eyes and noticed the entire windshield was gone and I could not breathe. There were only a few fragments of glass hanging on the perimeter edge.

Just take a breath! I told myself. I couldn't. Just breathe. I knew I would be fine if I could just breathe. I couldn't. Panic set in, just for second because I could not get a breath. Take a breath! I spit out hunks of glass. They were good size pieces. Take a breath! Fear. Then, I inhaled deeply for the first time and I felt relief. I was relieved that I did not have chest pains or problems breathing. That first breath came from deep within. It was a shaky breath. I heard Beth moaning a little but otherwise she was quiet. Somehow, I knew she was okay. I couldn't believe what had just happened. There goes my car. I knew it was totaled. I thought, I hope my son Jimmy takes a different route home. My car did a 180 degree turn in the air and was now heading northbound while it balanced itself on the guardrail to my right.

I wasn't in any pain whatsoever. I was groggy and very tired. Our car hit so hard that it ended up on top of the guardrail going in the opposite direction, but I did not learn this until months later. I was exhausted and I couldn't move. I could only turn my head slightly to the right. I lost my glasses and wondered where they were. I could barely move my head. I noticed my right arm was bloody and the blood was pouring down the entire length. I did not know where the blood originated from, but I could not move. I could only move my head to the right.

A few minutes later, I saw the outline of a man in front of my car. He was a distance from us, but I heard him clearly. He told us to hang in there. Help was on the way. I couldn't do anything and I didn't reply. I was so sluggish. I began hearing the sirens and I just rested.

I was at total peace. Months later, Beth and I talked about those moments waiting in the car. We both sensed this incredible peace. It is hard to describe what I saw. I saw this amazingly intense color. I saw fuchsia and magenta. Fuchsia is usually a more purplish color, whereas magenta is more reddish. Whatever it was, I was in total rest and peace. I just stared at that color. I heard these words in my heart. You're going to be fine.

I thought about that experience months into my recovery. I thought it was probably the lights from the emergency vehicles. Whenever I saw emergency vehicles at an accident scene at night, I looked for the color that was cast. No color was cast against the sky. Also, my crash happened in the middle of a sunny day which made the emergency vehicles lights cast nothing.

I talked to the fire fighters during the entire time they were cutting us out with the Jaws of Life. I asked them to try and locate my glasses. I figured that my head had swung sideways and that they were in the back seat. This one firefighter named Tim found them and put them on me. They were bent but to me, they were fine. The firefighters told me months later that my glasses were the least of my worries. I was being kept alive by a firefighter holding a bag of plasma. I was bleeding out. My blood pressure was dropping to dangerous levels.

Since I had my side window open, my left arm somehow was sandwiched between the metal carnage. I was totally unaware of the condition of my arm. The firefighters did not know how to cut me out. The engine block was resting on my stomach and I got a burn from that. I had no idea about all of this. I simply waited for them to do their work. I heard Beth moan loudly as they freed her from the wreckage. I was relieved that she was fine and on her way to the hospital. I thought I was fine except for the blood on my right arm.

One firefighter told me that they were going to put a blanket over me because they had to cut off the top of the car. I didn't care what they did. I replied, "Do what you've got to do." The blanket was very heavy and it was warm and dark underneath it. I was totally comfortable and at ease. I could have slept soundly under there. I could hear the cutting but I was not worried. I heard the words, "He is free!" I do not remember anything else until I was lying on a gurney at the hospital. I was told that Beth was lying next to me on her gurney. I couldn't see but I was aware of her presence. I saw three of my children- Julie, Breanne, and Jimmy the triplets, my brother-in-law Kevin, and my mom by my feet.

I didn't remember the ambulance ride because I coded on my way to the hospital. I first heard this from a doctor weeks later, and after that, I read it in the police report. That really shook me up. This could have been it for me. It was hard to imagine the reality of death. I learned, at a later date, that I coded a second time after my initial surgeries.

The first I remember a doctor doing was trying to put my big toe back in place. My large right toe was pointing to nine o'clock. I knew it was going to be painful. I was nervous, but helpless. Suddenly it popped into place. It was painless. He said, "That was easy. I hope the rest is that easy." That was the last thing that I remembered after saying goodbye to my family. I knew I was hurt, but I didn't think it was too bad. I felt so tired, I did not care what they did with me.

It was weeks later that I learned about the extent of my wife's injuries and my own. Beth had six broken ribs, a fractured left ankle, and a broken right leg. She did not have one scratch on her but she came in with glass slivers of all sizes all over her shirt, face, and hair. She did not have any internal injuries from the broken ribs.

I too was full of broken glass but I did not have any cuts from it. I even remember spitting out two hunks of glass from my mouth. I had twenty broken bones, but I did not have any internal injuries. Some bones were broken in more than one place. A few bones were turned to sand. My knee was missing bone. My surgeon told me that if a person suffered around nine broken bones there was always internal injuries or death. I was told by many doctors and nurses that some higher power or angel must be looking out for me. They began calling me, "The Miracle Man." I did feel blessed, but I would have felt even more blessed if I had totally missed the SUV.

Three days before the crash with Julie at the Met.

Two days before the crash with Breanne in Little Italy.

The night before the crash at Citi Field with Uncle Kevin and Jimmy.

An hour and a half before the crash.

A year later, sometime in 2016, my surgeon was using my history as a case study with his medical staff. He told them that with the way my left femur had broken in two places, and how both my arms had broken through the skin along with my knee shattering to sand, he wondered why I did not bleed out. He said he never saw anything like this. He should have bled out. He told them that they simply stopped the bleeding and cleaned me out that first night. There was so much major damage to my legs and left arm. He said, "Amazingly, he is still with us." My occupational therapist related this story to me at our next session. Over a sixteen-month period, they performed twenty-eight surgical procedures within twenty-two surgeries. I am scheduled for one more surgery at the time of this writing.

Here are some slides from my surgeon's presentation. There was nothing left of my right knee. In his 25 years seeing trauma, my surgeon said he never had seen a knee so bad. He said it was sand. He rebuilt it. He wished that he had given me a total knee replacement at that first surgery, but that was not the general practice. If he saw that again, he would have done the total knee replacement on the first knee surgery. I am stuck with plates, screws, and some kind of material that was formed to mimic bone that I lost. It is not as good as a total knee replacement. There are now risks to doing a full knee replacement. They would have to take all the metal out and allow the leg to heal for six months before going back in and replacing it with a new knee. There was a great risk of having the knee fused or amputation, if complications resulted. Here are my X-rays of what was left of my right knee. My surgeon said it was sand.

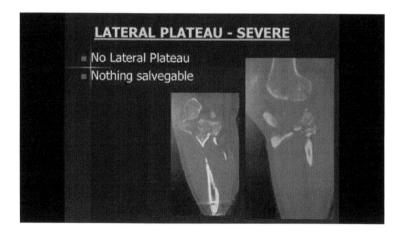

Here is the same knee now.

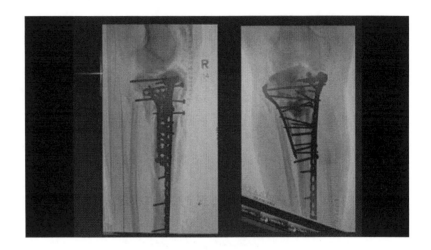

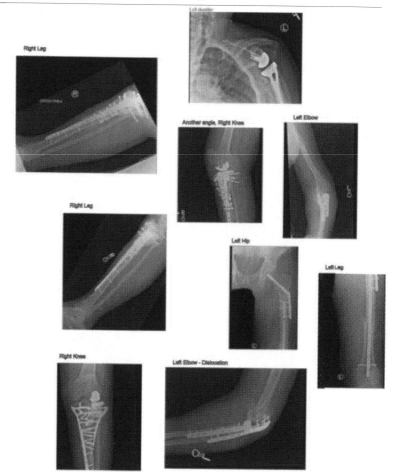

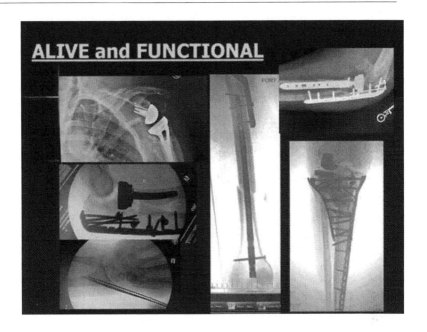

3 WAKING UP FOR THE FIRST TIME

Why was I in Denver? Why was I in the hospital? I was actually in St. Vincent's Hospital in Bridgeport, Connecticut, yet I was convinced I was in Denver. I have no idea how I came to that conclusion. Yet, I was one hundred percent convinced I was there. I could see the streets from my room. I learned later I was on the eighth and tenth floors of the hospital. The streets and neatly spaced homes were bright with sunshine. There weren't any familiar faces. People walked back and forth in front of my window. They looked busy.

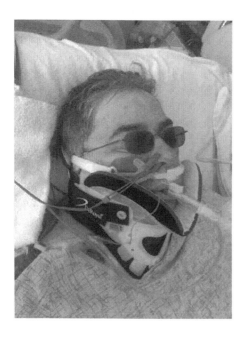

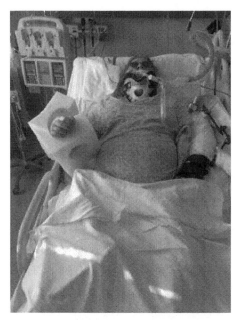

The only thing I was able to move were my eyes. I looked down and saw metal poles coming from my right leg. I later learned they were called fixators- a device providing rigid immobilization through external skeletal fixation by means of rods (*fixators*) attached to pins that are placed in or through the bone. My left calf had most of the right side missing. It was like someone took a sand wedge to the muscle. There was a gaping hole in the leg. It looked like a giant piece of raw steak.

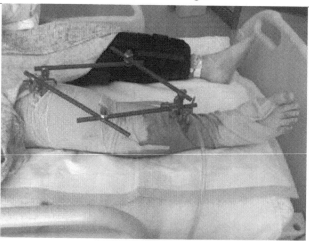

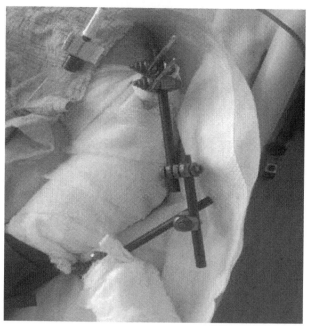

There were about four or five large pins coming out my left wrist. They were all pinned tight next to one another like a tight ball. Both arms were in traction. My neck was hot and uncomfortable with the brace. The hallway was busy with people.

I relaxed some as a young man came in and introduced himself. He was rather young, medium height with short brown hair. His smile put me at ease. I thought it was one of my old students who came back from college break and stopped by to say hello. He was the first doctor I met. I was in a confused state. Why was I here? What was I doing in a hospital room? In Denver?

I do not remember when, but the crash all came back to me. I looked at my arms and legs and figured that I broke some bones, but I thought I would be better in no time. My dreams were so vivid. I dreamt that I was in my father-in-law's Physic class back in high school. I felt terribly anxious. I had to speak to my children and warn them not to drive with their phones. I could not rest. I was anxious. I was in a panic in the dream. I had to talk to my children immediately and urgently persuade them not to use their phone while driving. I knew my accident was caused by a distracted driver.

What happened to my body? I had no idea I was hurt when I waited for help to come. I had absolutely no control of my body. I was literally stapled to this bed and I could not do anything about it. It was like this for weeks. I was trapped on my back. I was stuck on my back for the next four months before I was able to turn on my right side. For now, there was no movement. I would often wake up and find myself in a new room. I slept in short little naps and I spent most nights wide awake just waiting. I was sweating and perspiration built up on my neck brace. There was a time that I thought I was in a horror movie with a similar plot to Bill Murray's *Groundhog Day* movie. Somehow, I was in my own very real horror movie. Each day I woke up to repeat the same laboriously long, hot day. Was this hell? I wanted it to end. I thought death was better than this existence. I was tortured with pain, lacked restful sleep, and I endured uncomfortable heat.

I had a breathing tube down my throat for a little over a week- a week and four days. It seemed like months. My mouth was so dry. Thirst was raging for days. All I could do was wait. My friend Ted Josephson was there most of those first days. He visited me consistently for nearly four months, from April 17th until I came home which was August 13th. He was there the day they took the air tube out. I remember the nurse telling me that they were going to pull the tube out. I felt the tube slide up and out of my throat. It came out with such ease. I could not wait for something to drink. I had a raspy voice and could barely make a sound. "Can I have something to drink?" They would not give me something from a cup. I was given a little sponge with drops of water on it. I sucked that sponge dry. "More!" Sponge after sponge was sucked dry. "Careful. Don't give him too much," said one nurse. My friend Ted was the one giving me the sponges. I don't remember him being there, because I was so focused on the water.

4 HELL

There was a window in my room that looked out into the hallway. The hallway was darkened. There was a red glow from some lights that barely lit the hallway. My room had the same lighting. I had this terrible pain in my left shoulder. I could not wait for the night to end. I felt so alone. It was hot and I could not sleep.

Someone rolled my bed out of my room and up to a desk where a nurse was sitting. I wondered where I was going. She was looking over some papers. I just waited. It seemed like hours. The pain intensified. Why am I here? What are they going to do with me? The pain in my shoulder was intense and I could not think of anything else but relief. The nurse left her desk. I was alone again in this darkened hallway. I heard machines humming like my grandmother's old refrigerator. The noise and being all alone frightened me. What was going on? Are they going to do something with me? I could not wait until morning. The pain was fierce.

The nurse returned and she stood quietly by my left shoulder. She placed her hand on my shoulder and she began to dig her finger straight down into my shoulder. The pain was unimaginable. "Why are you doing this?" Silence. I waited. Nothing. The pain was steady and strong. I turned my head to see that she was staring straight ahead. Why was she doing this to me? I was being abused by the staff. I could not believe that this was happening to me. "I know what you are doing and I am going to tell on you when I get a chance." The pain and her presence persisted all night.

At one point, I must have dozed off. It was morning. The halls were filled with morning light and nurses. The mean nurse was gone. I was all alone back in my room. My shoulder was feeling some relief but not my heart and mind. Beth came in my room for her morning visit. I felt such a sense of relief when I saw her. "Quick. Close the door. Close it!" I couldn't wait to tell her. She had to get me out of here.

"What is it Vin?" She asked with concern. Her eyes and face were filled with pain.

"The nurses are abusing me." I told her all about last night. She looked horrified. There was a knock at my door. It was Joe the assistant pastor from my church. Beth shared with Joe what was going on out in the hall. Joe came into my room and I began sharing what was going on. He reassured me that the proper authorities were going to look into this. For the first time, I felt a sense of calm.

Joe shared with Beth that he had a similar experience when he was in the hospital for a long period of time. It felt good to have someone who understood me. He reassured me over and over again softly but firmly that everything was going to be fine.

He shared with Beth that I was hallucinating from all the heavy pain killer drugs. The best thing Joe did was reassure me that I was safe. He did not try to rationalize it or explain it away for me. I would not have accepted it. It was too real. I would have felt trapped in an awful situation with no one on my side. How can I convince people that I was in danger? I would have panicked even worse.

I do not remember the people in my hallucinations ever talking to me or anyone else. They were simply there. There were times when I mixed the hallucinations with real events. I asked my friend Ted who the guy was standing next to him. He reassured me that there was no one else in the room except the two of us. He told me a year later that I asked him that question at least five times.

Ted and I used to watch this show together when I was at the hospital about two guys going around the country looking for great steals at tag sales and antique places. I was one-hundred percent convinced that Ted and I were going to do the same thing when I got out. We were going to meet up with the guys on the show.

Hallucinations were frightening. I felt anxious and scared. I remember on many occasions of looking at the wall and seeing the whole wall melt like grape jelly. It was the color of light purple. I was terrified of what was happening around me. The worse hallucinations happened at night when I was alone. Sometimes I would see myself lying on air and looking down from the ceiling. Nothing was holding me but I was up by the ceiling. There were a few times when I noticed my son Vinny lying three feet below me. The room looked like a foyer and it was lit in an orange glow. No one else was in the foyer with us. He never looked up at me but I was sure it was him. Vinny, at the time, was going to school in Cyprus. I felt at ease when I saw my son with me. I tried to communicate with him, but he would not look up at me.

There were a couple of nights when four doctors came in my room to adjust my legs. In my mind, I thought they put me in one of those roll-away beds that folds up in half. I thought they were trying to close the bed with me in the middle of it. The pain on my legs was excruciating. They were probably adjusting the fixators or my bones.

On another occasion when my wife and two daughters were visiting me, a woman was rushed into a room near mine. There was a great commotion in the hallway. "She is bleeding! We must contain the bleeding!" Nurses were running by my room yelling directives. I began to shout to Beth and my two daughters. "Quick! Close the door! The air has been compromised. My air can't be compromised or I will die!" Somehow, I was convinced that if I breathed the air with blood particles in it, I would die. I was scared. I could not be rationalized out of my craziness. I know I scared Beth and the girls, but I learned that months later. I was so focused on my safety. Beth and the girls looked as frightened as I felt.

My dreams were exceptionally vivid. Some were scary but many were not. I had recurring dreams of painting pictures all in different orange shades while visiting Cape Cod with my daughter Julie. Once I was in Detroit surrounded by many Hall of Fame football players. I raced formula one race cars in another.

The hallucinations were a daily occurrence. I woke up and thought I was being kept in the cellar of a friend. Another time I awoke and found myself at my Cousin Doug's house. It scared me that I could not get out of bed. I wanted out of these places. I felt claustrophobic because I was in the basement, somehow attached to the bed against my will.

She was nose to nose with me and she was screaming, "Vinny! It is Sue Skoog.! It's me, Vinny!" She kept repeating this and I vaguely recognized her. Sue was one of my nurses and also a person I knew from when our children were in school together. She was just trying to get me back to reality. I was scared, but I did recognize her. I just could not communicate with her. I was trapped deep within my mind like I was stuck in a long dark tunnel. It did not settle me down.

My wife, other family members and friends told me that early on in ICU, they would enter my room and my eyes, were darting all over the room. They never focused on them. They were busy eyes full of fear.

My right arm was the first to regain some movement. I used to tug on my neck collar. It was uncomfortable and very hot. I was sweating and I needed relief. One night I heard the nurse from the station yell. "Leave your brace alone!" I must have said something and it was probably not my first time. She yelled to another nurse. "He is getting belligerent again!" I somehow knew when I was hallucinating. I thought to myself. I'd better stop or they will tie me down. I apologized and told them I am not usually uncooperative.

One night the nurse took my neck brace off. I felt the cool air on my neck. It was such a relief-heaven. During the night I had this terrible dream and I flinched my neck. The pain was electric and it reverberated throughout my body. Every time I saw the brilliant sun in my dream, my neck and whole body jerked. The next day, they put me back in the neck brace.

It wasn't day after day. It was week after week. They were long, hot days and sleepless nights. They were full of pain, fear, and loneliness. I was convinced I was in hell.

When I speak to high school students about my experience, I focus on the effects of the drugs on my mind. I tell them that it doesn't take much to alter the chemistry of our heads. I can't imagine getting stuck in that state for the rest of my life. I was horrified to find out that high school students now have "pharm parties"- pharmaceutical parties. They sneak pills from their parents' medicine cabinets. Everyone places the pills in a bowl and then they eat them like Skittles. It is insane. I tell them that I have never heard one person say to me, "Yeah, taking illegal drugs and large amounts of alcohol have been good for me. My life is so much better."

One night, I almost drowned. It was early in my stay at the second hospital- Gaylord Rehabilitation Hospital. I tried using my CPAP breathing machine. I started convulsing because I could not move and the addition of the full-face mask made me feel like I was trapped in the car. I waited at least a month before trying that again. The respiratory person set up my CPAP with water and he left my room. Suddenly, fear filled my heart as water began filling my full -face mask. He had put too much water in the reservoir. I was stuck on my back and I couldn't do anything. I frantically used my right hand to find the nurse's call button. Finally, I found it and a nurse answered. "What is it, Vinny?" I couldn't respond. I was drowning. I somehow got out a panicky garbled sound. "What?" she asked. She must have realized something was wrong by my unusual tone. Luckily, my room was next to the nurse's station. She came in and recognized the seriousness of the situation. I never used my CPAP again until I got home.

5 CONFUSED

One night a young nurse entered my room and sat in a chair at the foot of my bed. She had a faint smile on her face but her eyes were filled with tears. She told me that she was working in the emergency room when I was brought in. Then she began to cry. "We did not think you were going to make it." The reality of what she said did not fully impact me at that moment. She cried and cried and thanked God I was alive. I don't remember how long she stayed but she was there awhile. She spoke to me through her tears. I did not know how to process this.

It was always good to get visitors. Kevin Donovan, a teacher from my school, stepped into my room. He walked across my room to a chair on the right side of my bed. "Vin, how…" He looked at me and then the floor. His head moved back and forth as he crossed the room. He had a frightening look on his face as if in pain. He interrupted himself and kept swearing. "Oh, #$@! Oh, #$@!"

I had no idea how bad I looked to him or others. I wondered why he was acting this way. His eyes were huge. He kept looking at me in quick looks and then at the ground. He would not make eye contact. He put his hand over his mouth and shook his head. He didn't stay long and it was a long time before I saw him again. I figured that I simply had broken arms and legs. I would be fine once they healed.

A neurologist introduced himself one afternoon and he proceeded to open a tiny but long black box. It was long and narrow. The top opened on a hinge. He took out a very long sharp needle. It was shiny and silver. Really? What was the fancy box for? I thought. He asked if he could check me out. I obliged and he began poking my legs and arms. "Do you feel that?" I replied and wondered why he simply didn't just touch me with his finger. That needle hurt. He concluded his examination and told me that I would never move my left hand again. I was shocked by the news but also at the lack of sensitivity he showed. I replied, "Yes I will." He abruptly countered with, "No you will not." We went back and forth until finally he snapped back, "I know what I know." I thought to myself with tears welling in my eyes, you do not know who I know.

The doctor who performed the skin graft wanted to take a picture of his work on my left calf. It was the one that looked like a raw steak was hacked off my calf. He said it looked beautiful. It was anything but beautiful. It looked like a shark bite. It was a massive hole, red and deep. What he said next shocked me. "You were supposed to lose the left leg and your left arm." What the heck happened to me? I could not imagine waking up to see those parts missing. "You are lucky to be alive. You have a great surgeon- one of the best. We didn't think you were going to make it through the weekend." I could not process what he just said. Later, I found out that I was supposed to lose both my legs and left arm.

The doctor told me that they needed to do a fasciotomy on both my legs. A fasciotomy is a surgical procedure where the fascia (a sheath of tissue surrounding a muscle) is cut to relieve pressure to treat the resulting loss of circulation to an area of tissue or muscle. Fasciotomy is a limb-saving procedure when used to treat acute compartment syndrome. The trauma causes a severe high pressure in the compartment which results in insufficient blood supply to muscles and nerves.

I knew it was bad by the looks of my legs and arms, but the near-death news shook me. I do not remember when I saw the police report, but that news in black and white shook me to the core. It stated that I coded. I asked for clarification. I had died and the medical team brought me back. When? What happened? Me? That isn't supposed to happen to me. That could have been it? The full reality of the crash was sinking in.

I had to be careful with what I watched on TV. I could not watch the news. It was too negative. I was internalizing what I saw and I heard. My imagination was too vivid.

It was early May and I noticed the Mets were playing the Cubs. I was relieved to find a baseball game. This was something I could watch. I watched the game and felt totally confused. I could not remember how it was exactly played. I was scared. What happened to me? Was I losing my mind?

Transferring me from my bed to the wheelchair was very challenging. The nursing staff had to put this harness under me, which was very painful. They connected the harness to a machine called a Hoyer lift. It was an incredibly painful ordeal. Many times, the staff couldn't get the machine to work properly and I was left hovering over both the wheelchair and bed. It looked like those giant cranes unloading cargo off boats. I became very anxious. Pain would intensify the longer they held me in the air. It was a multiple person operation. One person was needed to keep my legs from falling downward. I can't explain the torturous pain it was on my legs. I thought I was going to pass out. One nurse snapped at me to take it easy and settle down. I was angered by her insensitivity. I could only last up to a half hour out of my bed. I often became nauseous and anxious. My blood pressure fell to low levels at times and I needed medication to settle me down.

I remember being wheeled to the gym at Gaylord for the first time. What was I doing here? It was full of people with missing limbs. Some were paralyzed in some capacity. Many were really old people who had suffered strokes and were in the process of regaining bodily functions. I looked at the scars on my legs and I said to myself that this wasn't fair. I had not ridden motorcycles my whole life for this very reason. I did not play football so I would not hurt my knees and pay for it later in life. That was drilled in me by my mother early in my life. I argued with her a lot over that. Now I was catapulted to the later end of my life with some serious injuries going forward. Suddenly, I felt like I was in my seventies- old and frail.

Gaylord Specialty Healthcare is a world leader in rehabilitation. Many patients come from all over the country to this facility. Here is a short description from the Gaylord website. "Gaylord is the only entity in Connecticut, and one of two facilities in the country, with Commission on Accreditation of Rehabilitation Facilities (CARF) International accreditation for all inpatient rehabilitation programs and additional specialty accreditation for our Spinal Cord, Stroke and Brain Injury Specialty Programs."

On another day, I rolled my wheelchair into the gym at Gaylord as usual. My physical therapist told me that we were going to work on a transfer from my wheelchair to the car using a board. The car is a full-size car with the motor missing and it is used for these purposes. I immediately rolled my chair over to the driver's side to get in. She told me that I needed to come around to the passenger side. I was simply on automatic. I was getting in on my usual side. I felt a twinge of loss at that moment. I wasn't going to drive for a while. I didn't think any more about it and obligingly rolled to the passenger side. The transfer was quite easy into the front seat. The instant I looked up from my seat, I burst into a deep weeping. It was almost like I was a spectator watching myself, because I kept telling myself to just let it out. Don't hold back. My physical therapist had enough wisdom to let me bawl and not interrupt. She handed me tissues and gave me room to grieve. I did not do anything else that half hour I was with her. I was shocked at the suddenness of this event. Will this happen one day while I am actually driving? Are there going to be other events like this that I can't control?

My left shoulder needed multiple surgeries. The full shoulder replacement was not holding and they tried one more surgery before they would have to replace the entire shoulder. I came back to Gaylord after the surgery with a special brace. I had a new nurse working the floor that day. She was in her early sixties. She took my new brace off to clean me without first consulting the head nurse. The nursing staff was livid because no one knew how to get it back on. I was sitting in my wheelchair getting ready to get some help to slide across the board back into bed. She was on my left and another nurse was on my right. Suddenly the older nurse put her arm underneath my left arm and yanked me onto the bed. I felt pain in my shoulder. I couldn't believe she did that. If she pulled my shoulder lose, I was looking forward to another major surgery- an entire shoulder replacement once again. I wanted to scream. I was furious. I turned to the other nurse and snapped, "I want x-rays! Now!" I also told her that I do not want the old nurse near me or touch me again. My heart was racing. My mind could not process this senseless act. Fortunately, the x-rays came back negative. The pain I felt was from my broken collar bone. One of the physical therapists was able to figure out how to put on the brace. When was this hell going to end?

The highlight for me was being able to go in the 90° swimming pool water at Gaylord. It was relieving to feel the heat on my entire body. I did not want my half hour session to end. It was also freeing for me not to have someone holding me up by the back of a belt they put on me.

In the beginning of September, I had knee surgery and elbow surgery the same day. It was autumn and I was now home for about a month. When I was recovering after surgery, I was told that I was going to need radiation done on my elbow. Radiation? I felt so violated. I had two days to prepare mentally for this. Radiation needed to be done within days of the surgery to be effective for keeping the bone from growing back where it was cleaned out. When I got to radiation, I was told that my surgeon wanted radiation done on my knee as well. I had no time to prepare mentally. What was I allowing to be done to me? I stared at these odd machines in disbelief. I spent the full day laying perfectly still while radiation was penetrating my body.

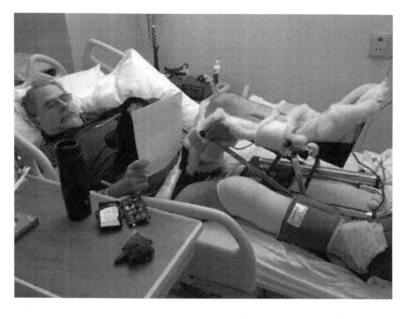

I was stuck on my back from April to August. I could never sleep on my back.

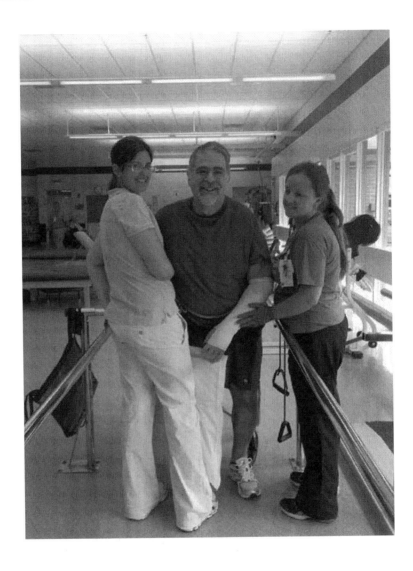

My first step with my two amazing physical and occupational therapists. One of the greatest and painful challenges was learning to walk again. Don't let my smile fool you. It was excruciating.

6 ANGER

Not only was this crash not my fault, but I was forced to accept major changes to my body and my life. I had two choices to make- die or learn to adjust. The hardest part was dealing with the words 'physical disability' and 'for the rest of my life'. I do not know what my future is going to look like. The only constants in my life now are pain and loss.

My mind was consumed much of the time with those four or five seconds before the crash. I am glad I did not swerve at the last second because that would have exposed Beth to a direct hit. As new revelations were made about the crash, a deeper sense of anger and injustice formed and I began to focus on that.

I found anger the hardest to deal with. It was harder than the surgeries, suffering physical and emotional pain, and for the losses to my body and finances. Being alone in my confused state was hell. I rarely slept. Most of my days and especially the nights were hot, painful, and confusing. The hardest part was that so many negative things were happening to me and I was forced to face new challenges.

Having to go through radiation treatment to kill abnormal bone growth angered me. It took all day to perform the procedure. I was left alone in the room with all these lines drawn on my arm and a giant machine pointing at one particular point. The procedure was repeated on my right knee. I had terrible thoughts running through my mind. What is happening to me? Why am I going through this? My body has been so terribly compromised. What will life be like in the future? Do I have a future or am I going to ride out the rest of my days in a bed?

The week following the procedure was filled with a burning pain throughout my left arm. I felt nauseous like I had flu-like symptoms for the entire week. The worst part was that the whole radiation process did not work on my arm. I still needed surgery to remove abnormal bone growth. I had a large bone mass on my left arm that needed cleaning out. The resulting surgery resulted in even more loss of movement and additional pain that was now continuous. My left arm lost almost all movement. It now felt like metal was tightly wrapped around my hand extending all the way up to my shoulder. This was now the new me-forever. Losing the use of my left arm was an unbearable surreal reality. Later in the year, I lost the use of my right hand as a result of a surgery. It looked like I would need more surgery to regain the use of my right hand. I was left with having both hands having as much movement as wearing a pair of mittens that I could not open fully. When I shook someone's hand, I would fist bump instead. I could not lift a cup of coffee to drink. In addition, I will have to take a medication for the rest of my life due to the blood clot in my right leg. My damaged joints were now left with arthritis.

Fighting with the insurance company over thousands of dollars stressed our lives. Just before I went back to work, my town asked for a release letter from my physician allowing me to go back. I am usually right on top of things.

I was asked to get a letter and by the following week June 19, 2017 two years after the crash, I got my letter. I was just about ready to begin work in late August, when I got a letter from my disability insurance company notifying me that they overpaid us almost $10,000. They wanted me to pay it back by a certain date. I called immediately to get clarification. This must be a mistake. There was no mistake. They said that since I was back to work on June 19, the July and August payments were now due back to them. I argued that I didn't start work on the 19th, I only got permission to go back. I wasn't going back until the last week of August and my first paycheck was not coming until early September. They quoted some rule that stated that the return to work began with the June 19th letter. They stubbornly refused to back down. There was absolutely no compassion in their voices. They began treating me as if I had stolen their money. This went on for months. I finally said that they were probably following the letter of the law, but they were missing the spirit of it. I asked them if they would treat their family member like they were treating me. No answer.

My wife and I were hesitant about going back. I did not know if I could do it. If I started my job and I could not do it, I would have to wait an additional six months without pay before I could go on the state's disability. I was feeling stress about going back and I had the additional stress of having to owe $10,000 hanging over me. I finally told the insurers that they were putting me through a lot of unnecessary emotional stress. I was making my case against them and I was ready to go to my lawyer. With the help of my physician and the town of Fairfield, the ordeal ended right before Thanksgiving.

I accumulated many unnecessary expenses. For example, the hunk of metal mass that was once my car was stored at a junkyard in Bridgeport for about a month while the investigation was going on. The junkyard passed on a $2,000 storage fee onto my lawyer who passed it on to me. Since my sick days took covered of my initial year of being out of work, my payments into my retirement plan were taken care of. The second year was the nightmare. I went on disability through my school's insurance. This gave me one more year to heal and improve and try and make it back to work. The disability insurance was sixty percent of my salary. The big change came to my insurance coverage. I lost the insurance for my family during my second year of rehabilitation because I was no longer getting paid through the town. If I wanted my old insurance, I had to pay somewhere around $28,000 to $30,000. In addition, I had to apply to the State concerning the loss of retirement for one year. Since I did not pay into my retirement, I had to pay out of my personal finances for the year I lost. I had to pay over $14,000 to reclaim my lost year. This was all happening as my four children were now graduated from high school and pursuing more schooling.

All of this paled when I consider the injustice I received from the law and the lack of concern I received from the family of the girl who hit me and caused such pain and agony for me and my family. The hottest anger reached all the way to my very core as this family tried to pin the responsibility of the crash on me. How did I get tangled up with such a self-centered family? This entire experience was a demonic nightmare. I just wanted to die. I did not feel lucky to have survived this crash. I felt cursed. I felt trapped.

I read the police report and I could not believe what I was reading. In the police report, the young woman, age twenty-one, was interviewed the day of the crash- April 17th. She stated that she, "did not remember anything about the crash." The report went on to state that on April 28th, the mother stated that her daughter "still didn't remember how it happened, but she believed the other vehicle had come into her lane." That was convenient and very selective. What a turnaround within a week. She went from, "I don't remember anything" to "I don't exactly remember how it happened. But, what I do remember is that the other vehicle was in my lane." It is interesting that she could not remember anything about the crash except her innocence. I could not believe the audacity of these people. Fortunately, the police did not accept her statement. The report stated that the young woman was totally at fault.

I think she did not remember any of the crash because she wasn't looking at the road. That crash must have truly startled her back to reality. According to the police report, the investigators did not find "any evidence of braking or evasive maneuvers." I remember trying to figure out where to go and holding to my lane. I froze with fright.

The next jolt came when I heard she had no insurance on the car. She was driving one of her dad's vehicles. The family was given a full month to show they had insurance. The mother claimed that it must be a mistake. Their vehicle was definitely insured. A month later May 18th, the mother brought an insurance card to the police department proving they had insurance. The police report stated that the mother brought an insurance card for another vehicle they owned. What was she trying to do? A police friend with over thirty years of service told me that she should have been arrested for fraud or for impeding an investigation.

It wasn't until late into the year that their own lawyer was made aware of the family's lack of insurance. According to my attorney, their lawyer thought his clients were paying for my out of pocket expenses. I wondered how he came to that conclusion.

Sixteen months after the crash, the court concluded the case against the father. It was August 2016 and the following are excerpts from the case. My lawyer was speaking. The judge ordered the father to pay $2,200 for some medical expenses.

5	Mr. Carbone is scheduled for his twenty-second
6	surgery next week. He is going to have another
7	surgery after that. He is probably never going to
8	work again. He -- the situation here and obviously
9	his physical handicaps now are permanent and he is
10	simply never going to be the same. This has been an
11	extraordinarily frustrating year for Mr. Carbone and
12	I'm sure the Court appreciated that. The Court has
13	been very, I think, attentive to the unusual set of
14	circumstances here.
15	Mr. Carbone is actually out of pocket
16	substantially more than $2200. There is -- if the
17	Court could allow me to just put it on record, Your
18	Honor.

5	Mr. Carbone is scheduled for his twenty-second
6	surgery next week. He is going to have another
7	surgery after that. He is probably never going to
8	work again. He -- the situation here and obviously
9	his physical handicaps now are permanent and he is
10	simply never going to be the same. This has been an
11	extraordinarily frustrating year for Mr. Carbone and
12	I'm sure the Court appreciated that. The Court has
13	been very, I think, attentive to the unusual set of
14	circumstances here.
15	Mr. Carbone is actually out of pocket
16	substantially more than $2200. There is -- if the
17	Court could allow me to just put it on record, Your
18	Honor.

19	THE COURT: Sure.
20	ATTY. BLOSS: He has lost income in the amount of
21	$40,000. His wife has lost income in the amount of
22	$14,650. He has lost the potential for summer work in
23	the total amount of $1,000. He's got additional
24	insurance expenses of $25,000 and had to buy a car at
25	on out of pocket cost of -- of $15,000 after this
26	collision.

His lawyer then responded.

```
                                                          5
 1          ATTY. ███████    Your Honor, if I may, my client is

 2     fifty-four years old.  He is a schoolteacher.  First,

 3     he would like to apologize actually to the family, the

 4     Court and the entire system for the situation.

 5          Unfortunately, there was a lapse -- a lapse in

 6     his insurance and it wasn't recognized until

 7     unfortunately after the accident.  He doesn't have a

 8     record.  This program is for people who are not likely

 9     to offend again.  He is not likely to offend again.  I

10     think he's been an outstanding citizen for fifty-three

11     and a half years until this incident happened.  He's

12     made the restitution the State asked for, the $2200 in

13     restitution.  I have the restitution, which I'll send

14     to opposing counsel.  I'm asking the Court to grant

15     the accelerated rehabilitation.
```

I wasn't sure why the defendant needed to apologize to
the court. Also, I wasn't sure what he meant by an apology
to "the entire system for the situation." I waited to read the
father's actual words.

```
16          THE COURT:  All right.  Does your client wish to

17     say anything?

18          THE DEFENDANT:  I'm sorry.  I didn't hear you,

19     Your Honor.

20          THE COURT:  Do you wish to say anything?  You

21     have a right to address the Court before I rule on

22     this request so I just want to give you your chance

23     whether you want to address the Court or not.  You

24     don't have to but I do want to offer you that right,

25     sir.

26          THE DEFENDANT:  I would just like to apologize to

27     all parties involved.
```

That was it. He apologized to all the parties involved. Who was he referring to? Did he have anything to add to my wife, myself or my children? This family never reached out to us in any way. His daughter ended up with a violation C.G.S. 14-236; Failure to Maintain Lane- cost $182.

So, what was this family really like? My brother Tony kept me informed about the family through Facebook and news reports. For starters, the young woman was posting about her 'car accident' on Facebook while she was recouping in the hospital during her one week stay. She was complaining that she did not have her phone and it was difficult to be without it.

I was very careful not to share the young girl's name with friends and family. I did not want them to respond to her in any way. I could see them tear into her and I did not want that. My brother and two other friends were the only ones who knew her identity. Somehow one of my colleagues found out her identity and was also following her complaints on Facebook. She responded in the text below. My colleague must have been so angered by this young girl's tirades that she accidently addressed her by a different name. I was made aware of this post two and a half years later. The girl never responded. It was a good post. It needed to be said.

Jen, as you recover I hope you are thinking about the couple you hit head on. Vin is still in the hospital today. He actually died the day of your accident but was resuscitated. He goes into surgery today. This will be #13. His father in law just passed away but he cannot attend. He has not been back to work to date but had triplets heading to college in the fall. Honey you got off easy. You should lose you license for 20 years. You and your phone almost killed my friend. You should be VERY REMORSEFUL.

Friends

The mother posted her own self-pity remarks. "No mother should have to receive the call I got last night. My daughter was in a car accident." She was right about that. My elderly mother worried about whether I was going to die and later about the extent of my injuries long term. It was devastating to my parent's and my wife's parents. Even on the anniversaries of the crash, the mother would post about the terrible crash her daughter went through. Was the mother somehow misguided about her daughter and confused over the insurance card mishap, or was she all about self-preservation? I began to wonder when revelations about other questionable behaviors began to come to light. The mother was convicted of an appalling crime back in 2010. There was a young seven-year-old girl dying of cancer in her town. She began collecting money for the young girl, but instead pocketed the money. Since the mother repaid the entire sum, her conviction went from felony to misdemeanor and she avoided jail time. There were more arrests that followed this woman in unrelated incidents. It certainly didn't reduce the heinous and self-serving nature of the crime.

I wanted to bring suit against this family, but they had no assets. I wanted them to share in some of the responsibility. It wasn't going to happen. It would have cost me at least $20,000 and they would have simply filed for bankruptcy. Then, I would need to hire a bankruptcy lawyer and a collections person after I got a judgement. Getting a judgement and collecting on it are two separate things.

I would have gladly cursed God at this point and died if given the biblical 'Job like' opportunity. I often asked Him why He did not just take me home. I contemplated taking my own life. It scared me where these thoughts were taking me. I began to think of ways, but I could not do this to my family. I wanted some relief. I could not take any more loss or any more pain. How can I live the rest of my life like this? I have nerve damage in all my limbs. I feel numbness from my knees to my toes. My feet feel like I have sand between my toes. My left arm varies in its pain, but the numbness runs from my elbow to my hand. I was scared. The life I knew before the crash no longer existed. I felt dead inside. I had the body of an elderly man.

These new life circumstances only anchored anger deep within me. It was as if anger was like a cancerous brain tumor that spreads through the lobes like the tentacles of a jellyfish. This type of cancer is inoperable because it weaves throughout the brain and is not contained to one area. Pain clouded my thinking and judgement. I learned that continuous pain interferes and shuts down all judgement. Would I ever find my way out?

The police could not prove 'scientifically' that the other driver was on her phone the time of the accident. They concluded that she had been on Snapchat three to five minutes before the crash. I called the leading detective in the case from my hospital bed at Gaylord and I asked him how he determined the time of the crash. He said the clock started at the time of the 911 call. I reminded him that there were no witnesses to our crash. He said that Route 111 is a very busy road. Someone should have come upon the crash scene quickly. I told him that I remember sitting in my car awhile before a man came into my view and reassured me that help was on the way. Later, I remembered another important point. Schools were out because of spring break that week and traffic was light. I was driving on the rural part of the road, not near the business area. It was no use. In my opinion, the time of the accident was not based on facts but rather it was a judgment call. Conclusions were determined by the time of the 911 call had been made and past traffic patterns. The obvious question was left unanswered. So, how can one account for this person being in my lane for a number of seconds? She had no health reasons to explain her crossover into my lane. It was no use. Case closed.

Detective Carbone's (personal) Investigation–
Date of the crash. April 17, 2015
Conditions the day of the crash: Sunny, warm, no leaves on the trees; it was Friday and the Monroe schools were not open due to their spring break. The crash occurred approximately at 2:00 pm. I was heading southbound on route 111. Due to the crash, my car landed facing northbound.

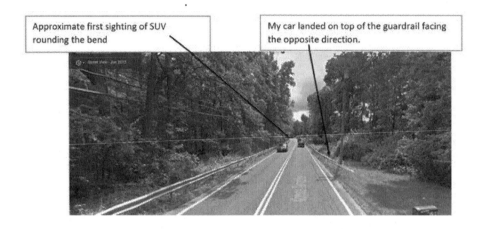

| Approximate first sighting of SUV rounding the bend | My car landed on top of the guardrail facing the opposite direction. |

Route 111 looking south

My brother drove the course for me while I used my stop watch. I clocked the time I first saw the SUV to the point of impact going 30 mph or 44 feet per second. At that speed and time of impact, it took 11.31 seconds. If the SUV were traveling at 60 mph, it would take 5.65 seconds or 88 feet per second.

Questions I have:

1. A GPS study should have been done on the other driver's phone. The location would be recorded when a text is sent or received in the phone. The footprints of those locations would determine that she was indeed traveling and texting.

2. The officer should have asked the young woman where she was coming from. If she was coming from her home, then this proved she was texting and driving because she lived more than 3-5 minutes from the crash scene.

3. What was she doing on my side of the road for about 4-5 seconds? This question was never answered.

4. She should have received a ticket for reckless driving. The detective did not think she should get that. How does this head on collision not result in reckless driving? What then qualifies for reckless driving?

Because of slack driving laws, she was not held to any responsibility. She got a ticket for driving in the improper lane, a $182 fine. It is my opinion that she was distracted. She was in my lane for a number of seconds, and she never applied her brakes.

I was mad beyond words. The young girl was home from the hospital eight days after the crash. My wife was in the hospital for two weeks. I was in ICU at St. Vincent's Hospital for five weeks. I was then transferred to Gaylord Specialty Healthcare on May 22nd until August 13th.

I lost a lot that year. I nearly lost my wife and my own life in the crash. I lost the use of my left arm and hand and the ability to walk pain free. I lost my car. I lost precious time with my four children. I lost out on seeing my son Jimmy have an incredible senior year in volleyball. He made second team for his division as the libero and his team made a good run for the states. I missed all their spring activities of our triplets' senior year including their prom, senior awards night, senior banquet, and graduation. It was hard for them that their father was absent from their graduation. They were mad. My son Vinny was away at school in Cyprus at the time of the crash. This was supposed to be such a care free enjoyable time in their lives and instead it was full of anxiety and stress.

I missed the rest of Jimmy's Senior Year of Volleyball

Senior Banquet- Spring 2015

The Senior Prom

Senior Awards

Graduation

My father-in-law passed away on June 5th. He was more like my dad then father-in-law. I knew him since I was about twelve. I had him as my high school Physics' teacher. I have been officially a part of the family one month shy of twenty-nine years. My dad died twenty years earlier and my father-in-law has been my dad. I missed his funeral. I could not take much more. But the worst was still yet to come.

I gained a lot that year. I got a blood clot in my leg. I gained a new shoulder, a partial hip, partial elbow, a new elbow and lots of metal plates and screws. I had ten blood transfusions. I have to take an antibiotic every time I visit the dentist for the rest of my life due to all the metal in my body. I had twenty-nine surgical procedures in twenty-three surgeries.

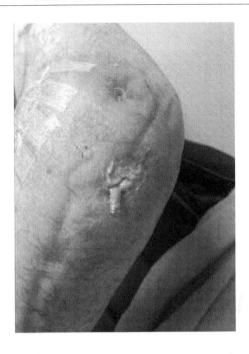

Here is a gross picture. A long screw was placed in one end of my elbow and it came out the bottom. The purpose was to try and hold the partial elbow in place. It kept slipping and this procedure didn't work and a whole new full elbow replacement was done. I felt like Frankenstein with all my scars and that one bolt coming out of my arm. I certainly walked like him.

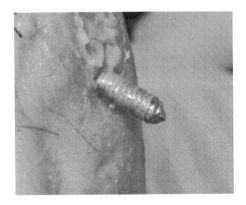

When Brian, my physical therapist, first saw the screw coming out of my arm, his eyes widened. He had never seen anything like it. My heart sank. He wanted the surgeon to look at it. He promptly made a call to the surgeon. My surgeon was unavailable so I had to see another surgeon. The same bewildered look on the doctor's face told me everything. Something was askew. No words were said. He quickly went into action shoving, pushing and jamming the screw back into my arm. I was given no anesthetic during this procedure. He pulled my skin over the screw. The screw resurfaced each time. After many pulls on the skin, I was relieved when he said he could not do anything else. I had to wait for my surgeon. I saw my surgeon the next day. He told me that nothing was wrong. He was trying something new. He needed the extra length for leverage, so he could pull it out easily once it healed the two parts of my arm. He never bothered telling others in the practice of what he was trying to do.

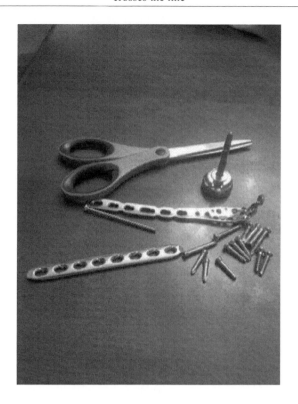

The hardware in the picture above was taken from my left arm and replaced with new hardware. Similar hardware is still in my right arm. The scissors are in the picture for perspective. I plan to make a wind chime from this and other hardware I collected.

November 2015 through March 2017 represented some of the darkest days of my life. I made the phone call to my school principal telling him I was going to retire and go on disability. I had hung up the phone and wept. I had stepped down from my position. After twenty-seven years, I was finished. My body was tired, in pain and I had no stamina. Two more major surgeries were being scheduled. I was convinced that I could not do the job. I began actively researching the pros and cons of total disability. I pretty much lost everything. I could barely walk and my left arm was useless and constantly in pain. My right knee feels like I am carrying a cinderblock.

When I had good days physically, I struggled with boredom. I had to do something. It was now a little over a year since the crash, the summer of 2016. I thought that I could somehow cut the lawn. I managed to climb aboard my tractor to cut the lawn. I barely was able to walk more than a few painful steps, but I wrestled my body onto the tractor. It took a lot of energy and balance to maneuver myself. Beth was not happy with me cutting the grass. I had to do something. Sitting around the house doing nothing but reading or watching television was getting difficult. I felt chained to my house and a prisoner to my wheelchair. I was determined to get my life back.

My first independent decision took me to my mower in the garage. Beth was against my decision. I struggled to pull my legs over the seat, but I felt liberated when I began to drive. I was alive again moving around the yard with ease. I steered the tractor with one arm, and it was hard. At least, I was doing something. It was exhilarating. It all changed in an instant. I took a sharp turn heading slightly parallel with the steep side hill. The mower deck was bent toward the hill and somehow it dug into the hill and stopped for a quick second. Time stood still. I was catapulted over the tractor. It was as if someone grabbed the back of my shirt and effortlessly pulled me up and over the tractor. I was suddenly looking down as I flew over the top of the tractor. Was this actually happening? It was surreal. I knew I was going to get hurt. I felt air all around me. The tractor kept moving once again rolling downhill- without me. We were both moving separately. In a second, I was in a dangerous situation and I could not do anything about it. The sudden thought of my left shoulder getting reinjured frightened me, but it was too late. I couldn't do anything but ride out the flight. Because of my limited arm movement, my arms were by my side and I was unable to stretch them forward to break my fall. I had no control of it. I looked like the guy at the circus who got shot out of the cannon headfirst with his arms by his side. My left shoulder and jaw hit the ground at the same time, gouging dirt and grass from the hill. I was sure my shoulder was injured. My face implanted into the ground and my body tumbled and skid to a halt. I frantically searched for the tractor. I managed to roll to my left, disregarding any pain as the tractor was rolling to my right. I was afraid I was going to get run over. I called for Beth and my first independent action was over. She was scared and not happy. The pain was intense but my fear was worse. I couldn't afford hurting my shoulder. I did not want major shoulder replacement surgery all over again. I was relieved when my surgeon checked out my shoulder and said it was fine later that week.

7 TRUST

Trust... Did I really trust God like the advice given in Proverbs 3? Sometimes my trust would fluctuate like the disciple Peter's. My heart and mind fluctuate depending upon the circumstances. One second, Peter is ready to follow Jesus anywhere but when a young girl simply recognizes who he is at the interrogation site of Jesus, Peter denies
Knowing Jesus. These experiences have a way of revealing our hearts. There were moments these past three years I felt more like the disciple Judas. Judas became disillusioned.
He was disappointed with Jesus because Jesus refused to embrace the earthly king role. Judas started planning other ways to get Jesus the role and finally just got disillusioned and made his own exit plan. Going through the past three years could have easily led me down the path to disillusionment. I did not buy into any of the poor arguments as to why this happened to me.

Somehow, God was with me right from the beginning in a tangible way. Something happened at the crash with the magenta, fuchsia color coming through the windowless car. I knew first hand that I was not alone and that everything was going to be okay- everything. I still do not know what it all means and I may never know but something happened that affected both Beth and me. I found throughout these three years that God was there in all my pain, emotional and physical. He was there in my deepest anger and disappointment.

On one occasion, three friends, Ted, Ray, and Everett, came to pray for me while I was in the hospital intensive Care Unit. As they prayed I smelled this incredible bouquet of roses. I did not see any, but the smell filled the room. I could not get over how strong the smell was. Suddenly, the head nurse entered my room and declared, "Guys, you are not supposed to bring incense or candles!" They were confused because they did not bring anything in nor did they smell the roses. They did not know what she was talking about. I was amazed. I never saw anything like this. If it weren't for the nurse, I would have thought it was some medication that caused me to sense this. By the way, I wasn't on anything at the time. I told them about the roses, and they laughed in amazement and at the nurse. Something was happening deep within me and I did not fully understand it. I think that is what happens when you have encounters with God's presence. He draws you into His intimacy with Him.

It happened again while I was at Gaylord Specialty Healthcare. There were six friends that came to pray for me. I was the only one who smelled frankincense. It is not uncommon for someone to anoint the sick with oil mixed with frankincense. It was so strong. I kept asking if anyone had it. No one had it or smelled it. I was amazed again. What was God saying to me?

One of the most amazing encounters occurred one Sunday in July at Gaylord. I woke up and I turned on Bethel music. Bethel Church in Redding, California has this amazing school of worship. This one morning, a young leader got up before the worship began and announced that if anyone wanted multiple baptisms, they should come up front to receive prayer. Multiple Baptisms? I had never heard of anything like this. I am a good student of the scriptures and I never heard of this. Since I trusted what Bethel was doing, I submitted to their prayer. I didn't fully get it, but I wanted more. I did not think any more on this. At one o'clock in the afternoon my friends Ray and Paula Lopez came for a visit. The first words out of Ray's mouth were, "Brother, I have a word for you. Multiple baptisms." I was baffled.

I responded, "Ray! What are you talking about? I never heard this phrase. I just heard that phrase a few hours ago." He explained that there are times where he feels waves of God's love hit him during worship at church. He simply rests and usually loses a sense of others around him. I never heard or experienced anything like that. The magenta, fuchsia color, roses and frankincense were my only encounters. This was all new to me. I never experienced anything so dramatic. I let him pray for me and I did not think any further about it.

I usually had trouble sleeping and that Sunday night was no different. It was around 2:00 am and I woke from a quick few hours of sleep. I do not recall how it all started, but I began feeling the love of God. I never felt anything so real. It did not let up. Each wave was stronger than before. I was weeping. Now, I do not cry let alone weep. My room was right next to the nurse's station. The night nurse came in my room. She saw me sobbing. "Vinny! Are you okay?"

"Yes," I replied.

"Are you in pain?"

"No."

She left the room and I continued on, feeling the love of God like I never had before. I began feeling a love for people in a new fresh way.

She entered my room a second time. "Vinny. Are you sure you are alright?" I nodded. "It is good that you are crying," she continued. "You went through a horrible trauma. This is healing for you."

"It's not that!" I pleaded.

"Well, what is it then?" she questioned.

"God loves me!"

With that, she quickly exited my room, and she never returned again that night. I laughed and continued on. Suddenly I saw a darkness. It was like seeing darkness within darkness. I can't fully explain what I saw. What I felt was the absolute lost state of mankind without God. It was so strong and scary. I knew once I went into that darkness, there was no turning back- ever. There was a terrible finality at this crossroad. I knew friends and family were in that darkness somehow, and they were not coming out. It was too late for them. I wailed. I was weeping something so deeply in my spirit that I never felt before or since. I couldn't continue in this state. I could not take this pain. It was too much for my spirit. Somehow, I knew in my spirit that I in some way tapped into the heart of God. It was God who was wailing- 24/7. I did not see Him, but I felt Him. I began praying for the souls of everyone I could think of. When I prayed for them, I felt a love for them I never experienced before. It lasted for a long time into the night. I feel like the multitude baptisms somehow connected me to the heart of God. I, in some small way, felt how God feels toward humanity- for every single person. It was not something I could endure for very long, and yet I knew this is how He feels all the time.

I wondered if these experiences were preparing me for something. They seemed so random. I found later that these experiences were preparing me to deal with my greatest challenge- inner healing from intense anger. There were two unrelated memories that came to mind that helped me process the next step in my healing.

There was a memory that came to my mind three years after the crash. I found it was somehow connected to my situation. It was a hot, humid Sunday morning service back in the early 1980's. It was oppressive. The air was thick. During the Sunday morning service, an elderly man collapsed. Heart attack? Stroke? Confusion. Fear. People gasped and someone quickly called for an ambulance. The man who collapsed was Ray Whittles. He was a short, small framed elderly man in his mid to late eighties. We were all shocked, because we knew him as our beloved Uncle Ray. He was known to all affectionately as Uncle Ray. I loved whenever he prayed. God was real. Uncle Ray was a successful businessman who had been able to retire comfortably. Through the two decades I knew him, he was always meeting the needs of those in and out of church-quietly underneath the radar of being seen. He was ministering spiritual and physical needs for many decades before I came to this church. He was a spiritual pillar in the church. A few days before he collapsed at church, Uncle Ray was visiting a person in need. Just after his visit, he was mugged and robbed.

We came to find out why Uncle Ray collapsed. He had merely fainted in church due to the heat and for lack of food. Lack of food? It wasn't a heart attack or stroke. Uncle Ray was fasting and praying for the person who mugged him. He wanted the person to experience the love of God. I was stunned at his graciousness, mercy and forgiving heart. It was an act of love I never experienced before, nor one I fully grasped. Is forgiveness an option? Are Jesus' words on forgiveness for real, or are they simply black ink on a white page?

Another example of the transforming power of forgiveness, for me, was seen in the life of Sylane Mack. Little did I know that her life story would impact my own inner struggle years later. I met Sylane in 2010 at my church when she shared her personal story of growing up in a family surrounded by intense physical, emotional and sexual abuse. The sexual abuse began when she was three or four years old. Her mother stood in the bedroom doorway watching her husband rape little Sylane. Sylane endured years of this behavior by her father and also later by her oldest brother. She had nowhere to hide from these sick and twisted family members. There were times her father would grab Sylane by the hair and hack off chunks of it with his hunting knife. His drunken rage was the norm and he took out his anger on everyone. He once held the barrel of his loaded rifle at his wife's head in one drunken rage. There was another gun incident when he was taken away by the police after a standoff. The inner rage and intense hatred grew inside of her, while her secret was hidden from outsiders. Sylane was away from home as much as possible to escape the hell she was living in. She hitchhiked one day only to be raped from the stranger. She began to wrestle with suicide.

I would have been fine if she had said she had killed her father with a gun. That would have been the normal reaction. Instead, Sylane had encountered God in the midst of her dark world and she chose to forgive. My mind shouted, "No. Don't let them get off that easily." I believe she needed to silence them all. Forgiveness is not natural nor logical, and, at first, Sylane agreed.

When Sylane finally shared her pain filled experiences with a trusted adult- her youth leader Raylene, Raylene responded with three words. "Now, you forgive."

Sylane responded, "I was totally shocked. Dumbfounded. Blind-sided. Angry. Confused. Hurt. I just stared at Raylene. Every natural instinct within me was screaming out with a burning force and an even hotter indignation, "No!"[4]

It was a process for Sylane to see the wisdom and accept the gift God was offering her. "I could choose to turn my back in defiance. I could choose to close my hands to God's gift... and choose to form them instead into fists to be shaken at God in anger for all that had happened to me. I could choose to harden my heart and hold onto all that hatred, the pain, the brokenness and bitterness that came as natural consequences of my experiences. Or I could choose to be a bucket to be filled with the gift of forgiveness that God was offering to me."[5]

Her book *Convinced* is a story of the transforming power of God in her life. It is a story of a God who enters our hell with his justice and love, through the cross, in order to make all things new again. Is this really possible? There is no other explanation for the total transformation of Sylane.

The power of God not only transformed her heart, but it defeated the evil in the lives that almost destroyed hers. Sylane wrote, "And although I do not comprehend it fully by any means- nor could I at the moment—I believe that not only were spiritual chains broken off from me that night, but that through God's Spirit and His enabling me to extend His unbelievable, counter-intuitive, life-changing forgiveness to others, there were also layers of spiritual chains broken off from my abusers—especially from Mom and Dad. The enemy of God could no longer use me...could no longer hold them bound by any chains of hatred and judgment that came from me. My condemnation of them was gone. Their wrongs were still real. Still ugly and evil. But I would no longer be pointing at them as their accuser. Instead, by God's loving, freeing power, I opened my hands to accept God's gift of forgiveness to cover their sins just as Jesus had done for my sins...for *all* sins on the cross."[6] Forgiveness, for me, was not a one-time act. New revelations about my situation brought back to that murky pit. In fact, it wasn't something I could do without supernatural help. Each time, it came down to an act of the will.

I was inspired by these real examples of transformed people. Could I forgive like them? People would often say, "Karma, Vin. It will come back to them." I did not want that, but there was another side of me that felt otherwise. I battled in my heart and mind. I was not like Ray Whittles or Sylane Mack. I was more like the disciple Peter who missed it, too. The disciple Peter missed the heart intention of God when he said was willing to forgive seven times in the Gospel of Matthew 18:21-22. Peter, being a good Jew, knew that seven was the number for completion. Jesus responded with the phrase, seventy-seven times. What did Jesus really mean?

Ann Spangler and Lois Tverberg's book *Sitting at The Feet of Rabbi Jesus* helps us understand the heart intention of God. There is a chapter titled, "Stringing Pearls." It was a rabbinic technique well known throughout the centuries. Rabbis would often quote part of the scriptures to make a point. What isn't said had a greater impact than what was said. This was practiced in a community that really knew their Bible. For example, one older man was angry with this younger man. The older man rebuked the younger by stating, "I have raised children and brought them up."[7] It does not make sense to us. The younger man knew exactly what the older man meant because he knew where the quote came from. It is from Isaiah 2 and the rest of the verse states, "But they have rebelled against me."[8]

What did Jesus mean by the phrase "seventy-seven times"? There is only one passage that has that phrase in the entire Bible- Genesis 4:24. "I have killed a man for wounding me, a young man for injuring me; If Cain avenged seven times, then Lamech **seventy-seven times.**" As Spangler and Tverberg state, "Lamech was a descendent of Cain who had inherited his forefathers' murderous instinct, but who, in his shocking lust for revenge, outdid even Cain. Anybody who crossed Lamach would have been paid back big time- not just seven times, but seventy-seven times! In scripture, seven is a significant number. It symbolizes completeness. But Lamech lusted for vengeance that went far beyond completeness. Once you catch the reference, you understand the contrast Jesus was making. He is saying that his followers should eager to forgive as Lamech was to take vengeance. Just as Lamech was vowing a punishment that far exceeded the crime, we should let our forgiveness far exceed the wrong done to us."[9] Jesus was actually revealing the heart of God. I do not know anyone who lives like this. Our forgiveness should far exceed the wrong done to us? Really? That's the point. Man needs a change of heart. Forgiveness is an act of the will that opens us up for God to change us with a heart full of mercy and grace. That is what happened to Sylane. Read her story to find out what happened to her and her family. Forgiveness is not something to be done a number of times to show good effort, but rather a heart full of mercy and grace.

I made a choice to forgive. I had to forgive the girl, the family, and myself. Could I have reacted differently in the car? Why did this happen to me? Forgive? It was harder than any surgery, physical rehabilitation, or personal loss. It was an act of my will. It is an act I needed to repeat every time anger and bitterness inflamed my heart and mind. This does not mean everything is okay. It isn't okay that I had to endure all of this. The hardest challenge is feelings of bitterness on days when I experience lots of physical pain. I do not need to read in the Bible about some rule I must accept and grit through. I needed to revisit that night in the hospital where the love of God showered upon me and through me. It is the only way wholeness can be regained. I have experienced some of that wholeness, but I still need more.

Not everything that happens is the will of God. God did not stop Cain from killing his brother Abel. God warned Cain that sin was at his door. Cain had a choice to make. Freedom. Real love allows for real freedom. With freedom come consequences, good and bad. While it seems that the death of Abel and the injustice of it was left unanswered, it wasn't. In fact, the injustice of Abel's death was answered. Revelation 13:8 states: "... And all that dwell upon the earth shall worship him, whose names are not written in the book of life of the Lamb slain from the foundation of the world."

This world is full of injustices- Sandy Hook, sexual exploitation, innocent lives taken as a result of D.U.I. drivers, etc. Just read the papers or watch the news. Somehow, someday all wrongs will be answered for. But, can I really forgive?

To be honest, the struggle between constant physical pain, loss and bitterness has made me consider ending it all. Forgive? It was scary where my mind was taking me. I was struggling with despair. The longer I perceived lack of improvement, the deeper I sank. Forgive? The reality of long-term pain and permanent disability over an incident that was thrust on me made me go to dark places. Forgive? It was easy to be selfish and think only of myself. Pain has a way of doing that. Forgiveness is a choice. I found that I was met each and every time with a power greater than me.

A thought came to me. Can I trust God to make good of this evil situation? Another thought entered my mind. What kind of legacy do you want to leave your children? I want my children and future grandchildren to be overcomers. Life has many challenges. We all have experienced some sort of injustice. We all face tough challenges. Everyone goes through difficult moments that demand a choice. We can choose life or death. A simple decision to escape life through drugs or other damaging choices or do I accept life's challenges and make life giving choices. What will my decision to forgive and choose life have on my decedents?

Let me return to my life's verse in Proverbs 3:5-6 (NIV) [5]"Trust in the LORD with all your heart and lean not on your own understanding; [6] in all your ways submit to him, and he will make your paths straight."

It is hard to understand why this happened. I trusted God my whole life and I desired to know God more each day- well most of the time. Beth and I were serving together consistently in the church. I had questions, but I never doubted God's love.

Some have quoted the Bible verse to me where it says, "God will give you only what you can handle." First of all, the Bible does not say that anywhere. Second, it goes against the very nature of God as if He contemplated the number of broken bones I could take.

But God does discipline those He loves. He does, but we usually think of a father full of anger. Have you ever been disciplined by a loving father? A loving father would not break your arm to teach you a lesson. There are many Christians who believe God is ready to judge people for their evil. There will one day be a day of judgement, but it will be 'one day'. In the meantime, God's love for the entire world has not changed. He desires for the whole world to know Him. John 3:16 "For God so loved the world that he gave his one and only Son, that whoever believes in him shall not perish but have eternal life."

I also don't agree with some Pastors who give more power to the enemy when something bad happens. The enemy only has power if the believer opens life to him.

We live in a world where God gives mankind total freedom because love demands it. God loves; He is good and He is in control. Some people think that everything is predetermined. This reminds me of the joke about the minister who fell down the stairs. He broke his leg and said, "I'm glad that's over with." Tension between the freedom found in His love and His control is hard to grasp. Here I sit with nerve damage in both my arms and legs. I do not walk with ease of movement and stability. Pain often fills my steps in varying degrees. My left arm and hand have little to no movement. There is a numbness that runs from my elbow to the hand. I type with one finger. I cannot play catch with my boys. Yet total freedom is the only condition where true love can be experienced and demonstrated. Freedom allows for the possibility of rebellion with all its consequences. It is this apparent paradox where God is in control and all-knowing and yet mankind is free to make choices good and bad that we live in. Mankind choose a course that brought about a fallen world where evil and injustice occur seemingly unchecked. This needs to be repeated. God warned Cain about the sin that was about to overtake him if not dealt with. God did not jump in and save Abel and yet He did. As stated in Revelations 13:8, God dealt with the consequences of our choices before the foundation of the world.

Charles Spurgeon once said, "O dear friend, when your grief presses you to the very dust, worship there!" When I feel bitterness and anger pressing into the very dust, I worship. When I experience pain and loss, I worship. I feel shame when people look on my awkward arm or hand movements. I would rather hide my weakness or pretend it is not there. Yet, God wants you and I to relate to Him with our weakness fully acknowledged. My daughter Julie said to me, "Dad, don't focus on what you lost. Rather, focus on what you gained."

2 Corinthians 12:9-10 [9] But he said to me, "My grace is sufficient for you, for my power is made perfect in weakness. Therefore, I will boast all the more gladly about my weaknesses, so that Christ's power may rest on me. [10] That is why, for Christ's sake, I delight in weaknesses, in insults, in hardships, in persecutions, in difficulties. For when I am weak, then I am strong."

I am determined to use my weakness and lay my weak hands on people in prayer. It is my hope that the power of God would come through my weakness. I am contending for my healing and theirs, as we touch heaven together.

This event has challenged my faith in a good God. These events have also deepened that conviction of His goodness. Now, I marvel at the smallest things. I see a couple holding hands or a young child run in circles trying to catch a butterfly. I took so much for granted from the small nerves that control my hands and feet. I wonder if people thank God for these simple pleasures. I know I did not. I took these events for granted. I now thank God for what I can do and for what I used to do. Our bodies possess numerous gifts that enable us to enjoy this world. When I focused on each of my body's senses, I began to wonder with great gratitude at the mystery of life's experiences. I now find myself concentrating on the deep colors of my wife's flower garden with amazement. I love the smell of a wood fire in our fire pit and feeling the warmth of the flames on my face on a chilly night. I am content just sitting close to my wife sharing a moment and feeling the warmth of her body close to mine. I have seen the look of tender love in her eyes as she has reassured me that she is just glad that I am here. I have had two of my best friends and my brother tell me with tears in their eyes that they are simply glad that I am here. I have received more love through all these experiences.

Why did God allow this crash to occur? He is not angry. He wasn't teaching me some life lesson. Mystery, yes. He is the one who created the tiny nerves to the grandest galaxies. Sometimes I feel so small and insignificant. This, itself, is a mystery that a God so great would care for humanity or even little me. But that is precisely the Good News. It is too good to be true that our God would seek us out for intimacy. Lois Tverberg states in her book, *Walking in the Dust of Rabbi Jesus*, "In Christ, God willingly suffered as an innocent person to gain forgiveness for our sins." [10]God did this so we could intimately know Him. Job struggled with his own suffering and his friends were no help. His questions were not answered. But in his intimacy, Job understood God's great compassion for the hurting.

Tverberg explains that living within a paradox is difficult in the West because we want to resolve the conflict by rejecting one side or the other. She quotes Marvin Wilson when he writes, "The Hebrew knew he did not have all the answers...He refused to over-systematize or force harmonization on the enigmas of God's truth or puzzles of the universe...The Hebrew mind was willing to accept truths taught on both sides of the paradox; it recognized that mystery and apparent contradictions are often signs of the divine." [11]

We live in a world that has fallen with all of its consequences. Life is a mystery. I still pray for God's protection. In the Lord 's Prayer, Jesus taught his disciples to pray that they be delivered from the evil one. The consequences of this fallen world affect us all- pollution, credit card theft, mediocre workmanship to name just a few. This is why Jesus taught his disciples, "Thy will be done on earth as it is in heaven." As Christians, we are to influence every area of life bringing God's Kingdom and ruler-ship. This means we bring His goodness, love and healing so life on earth resembles heaven.

I am still contending for further healing. I am using this experience to talk to young people about the need to drive with their full attention. I became a speaker for **We Save Lives** organization. I believe there will be much good coming out of this evil- God's specialty.

James 1:2-4

"Consider it pure joy, my brothers and sisters, whenever you face trials of many kinds, because you know that the testing of your faith produces perseverance. Let perseverance finish its work so that you may be mature and complete, not lacking anything."

Reread it carefully. It is not that it is pure joy while experiencing trials, but rather it is pure joy when you lack nothing.

8 THE NEXT STEP

I went to the state capitol a few times to meet with members of the Transportation Committee to try and improve laws concerning texting and driving. I met some very nice, caring State representatives. Connecticut has some of the strongest texting laws in the nation. Some states do not have texting laws or they have very weak laws. The problem we have is trying to get the authorities to catch people in the act. We have laws in this state but not enough enforcement. I am writing my story so people would be aware of the lives that are changed forever. This could have all been avoided if people had begun taking the responsibility of driving seriously. Driving is not a part time activity. It demands our full attention. I used to joke and say, "Would you want your surgeon preoccupied with something else while they operate on you?" Of course not. We would be appalled. Yet, more lives are at risk every day and we just accept it. Leadership is needed at the state and federal level to make our roads safe again. It is not about raising fines, but rather penalizing people by getting them off the road for a period of time. Consequences are needed.

I also became a member of the *We Save Lives* organization that Candace Lightner founded. She was the founder of M.A.D.D. (Mothers Against Drunk Driving), as well. What I admire the most about Candace is that she changed our culture and our attitudes towards driving under the influence of alcohol. The mentality changed from the boys will be boy's mentality to true accountability. That same kind of change needs to happen with using phones and other hand held devices while driving. It is harder because car companies install WIFI in cars. That's like putting an open bar in the car. Both are driving under the influence. The epidemic of those texting is worse because of the numbers and it happens all day and night. Paying a fine doesn't change attitudes. Taking licenses away for a month or more will get people's attention. I loved talking to high school students about my experience during the spring of 2017. I saw many of my old students. It seemed to impact many of them.

Here I am in Hartford speaking at an open forum before the Transportation Committee.

Overwhelmed by God's Love

My family and I were overwhelmed with the outpouring of love. I had an incredible amount of love showered on my family. I am forever grateful for the way God met our every need. My brother-in-law, Kevin Magee, came to live with my family right from the start. He cared for our children, becoming both mom and dad to them. He managed their busy senior year schedules. He brought laughter and care into our home during a very difficult time in our children's lives. The Monroe community was amazing with their generosity. The school community paid for all of the spring senior year functions- senior prom, senior banquet, and senior trip. My daughters had their nails and hair done for their senior prom. The girls already had their dresses but the community was willing to purchase these, as well. Joe Kobza, the Principal, offered to help my son Vinny fly home from Cyprus. Vinny decided to stay in Cyprus until the end of his term. We were amazed at this gesture. They set up meals called 'The Food Train' for three months. People either dropped off incredible meals or they gave gift cards to local restaurants. I heard about these meals while I was up at Gaylord Hospital.

My school family from Fairfield Woods Middle School were equally generous. They hooked up with The Food Train. Bea Bagley and Margaret Richter, my team teachers, got the whole school involved in sending me a musical video to cheer me up. They plastered my hospital wall with personalized messages from my students. In addition, the Fairfield Woods Middle School had a fundraiser with special music by two fellow teachers- Jeff McHugh and his band and Jeff DesRosier and his band. I saw parents there from my first year of teaching. Tina Bengermino, another teacher, had students decorate rocks. She came up to our house with others to plant flowers around our yard. Many of my old colleagues from North Stratfield School and old retired friends came out in my support.

My niece Sarah and her future husband Ray set up a 'Go Fund Me' page. Many of my cousins and friends generously contributed. I even had friends from high school days contribute. I was refreshed by my cousins' visits, especially those who drove great distances to see me.

My church, Valley Shore Assembly of God, gave us money towards our expenses. Pastor Joe Lyons took me to rehabilitation appointments. He lived an hour away and yet he drove me to rehabilitation appointments once or twice a week for months. He drove an hour to my house and then forty minutes to the rehabilitation hospital for my outpatient physical therapy. Then, he would drive me home and then another hour to his home. Art Cote and Joe constructed ramps for my back deck for my wheelchair. Joe also added a railing to my cellar stairwell. David and Linda Long spent many days at our home doing plumbing and tree work. Janet LeBoutillier and Barb LaBonte helped Beth and I navigate through the pathway to much inner healing.

Pastor Dan McCandless of Black Rock Church came up to our home with a group of guys to repair our deck.

Two very close couples gave us substantial gifts from their savings.

More Evidence of God's Presence

God has met with each one of my children throughout this entire time. My son Vinny was met with the love of God on the day of the accident. It was one of the strongest encounters of His love and presence in his life. Because of that encounter, Vinny was able to preach for the first time on April 24th. It was exactly twenty years to the day that my father died, and here he was preaching for the first time. I felt like this was very significant for our family. The enemy did not win twenty years ago and he was not going to win here.

Beth and I have been touched by the love of God through everyone. My best friend, Ted Josephson, was at my side throughout my stay at St. Vincent's Hospital and Gaylord Hospital. I would not have made it without him. My other best friend, Mark Behm, was away on business overseas when he heard the news. When he landed in Philadelphia after being in Japan on business, he quickly checked in at home and he made the three plus hour trip up to see me. I wasn't aware of his presence on that trip. My wife's best friend from college Alice Schmidt drove up from Baltimore to stay with Beth's mom and visit us. She stayed for weeks before heading home to be with her family.

I remember noticing so many people at Gaylord had no visitors. I felt that inner voice in me. I had so much love shown to me. I was reminded to reach out to those around me that had no one. The world is full of lonely people, not just at Gaylord.

Beth and I celebrated our twenty-ninth anniversary while at Gaylord. That number struck me. It was a lot of years. How many years have I just taken her for granted? I apologized to her for taking her for granted so much of the time. Much healing and tenderness came about as a result of this time period.

Real healings were achieved that had nothing to do with the crash. The trial brought me to a place of real healings in my relationships. I learned to love and that went beyond the crash. My brother, Tony, and I grew very close through this time. I apologized to my son Jimmy for my quick tongue and lack of patience. It was nice to see that distance between us mended. I am grateful that he experienced healing in our relationship. So many people get to this point at the end of their lives. It is nice to see him thrive going forward in his own relationships.

I am forever grateful to Beth. She used to say to me when I was talking to one of our children, "I don't have any problem with what you said. It is the way you say it that is wrong." It was because of her that I went to New York Tuesday, Wednesday, and Thursday just before the crash with each of my children. She always encouraged me to make heart connections with each of our children. I am forever grateful for her.

A year and three months since the crash. Our 30th wedding anniversary at the New York Botanical Gardens- 2016 The wheelchair was not in the picture.

Breanne, Julie, Vinny and Jimmy 2016

9 UPDATE

In the spring of 2017, I visited three local high schools to share my story. I became a member of We Save Lives, an organization dedicated to educating people about the dangers of driving under the influence of alcohol, drugs, or driving distracted. I loved talking to high school students about my experience, especially since I saw many of my old students. In many ways, I wrote the book for them. I don't want them to hurt themselves or anyone else when this could have all been avoided.

Here I am sharing my story at Fairfield Warde High School in the spring of 2017. I am with a senior student who was one of my old students.

I made it back to work in September 2017. It was two and a half years from my last work day. I hobbled into school with my cane. By June 2018, I was walking without the cane. My students were always helpful, especially a group of girls in my homeroom. One student would ask me every morning she entered homeroom if I needed any help with anything. I wasn't thrilled with the thought of being with a new team of 110 middle school students in my condition. I wondered how they were going to accept a teacher who rode an electric cart and had one arm that resembled a T. Rex dinosaur arm. Middle school students are known for their keen ability to point out differences in one another. Somehow, they were accepting of me, at least to my face. They are also very funny. I had this one student who imitated my walk and my bent arm.

As my legs got stronger, I began to wonder if I could do some of the activities, I never thought I was going to do again. Chris Verras, a great paraprofessional, and others had encouraged me to give the Starlab Portable Planetarium a try. He helped me set up the Starlab Planetarium. This is an amazing teaching tool I had used for over twenty years. The difficulty for me is trying to work the planetarium with one arm. It was worth the pain of climbing in and out to see the excitement on the student's faces.

In May 2018, I took a small group of my students to an underground mine in New Jersey. The was a major achievement due to all the walking I had to do. A parent carried a folding chair for me, so I could sit and take breaks. I could not even consider doing this trip back in the fall when I was walking with a cane. In June, I felt strong enough to try an actual geology dig up a steep hill in Trumbull. I took a small group of students to Old Mine Park in Trumbull. It was very difficult getting up the hill, and it was almost impossible coming down, but I made it. Again, I had a parent carry a folding chair so I could make the walk with frequent breaks. It was worth the pain and effort to see the students enjoying themselves.

June 2018 Old Mine Park Trumbull, Connecticut

My final school was achieved on the last day of school. It was a personal achievement to take back all that was stolen from me. I was not absent one day due to illness. I was exhausted by the end, but I made it. It gave me great satisfaction to walk out of school that last day, and without a cane.

My last personal goal was to go on an extended walk with my wife. I accomplished this on my 32nd anniversary in July 2018. My legs are still improving.

It was gratifying to be able to take an extended walk that day with minimal pain. I was encouraged thinking that more walks with Beth were coming.

And finally, I did the unthinkable just a year before. I walked out towards the shore with Beth at Long Beach Island in July 2018. The last time I was there, I was in a wheelchair.

My friend Ray Lopez shared the following verses from Hebrews 12:12-13. "Therefore, strengthen your feeble arms and weak knees. Make level paths for your feet, so that the lame may not be disabled, but rather healed." The weak arms and weak knees caught my attention. I appreciated the encouragement of the lame being healed, but it was the following verses that captured my attention. Hebrews 12:14-15 "Make every effort to live in peace with everyone and to be holy; without holiness no one will see the Lord. See to it that no one falls short of the grace of God and that no bitter root grows up to cause trouble and defile many."

I am convinced that we all need healing from bitterness and offenses. Being in a fallen world opens us all up to experience hurts and disappointments. We have all experienced injustice of some kind large and small. My experience with injustice was more extreme than some, but sadly, others have had it worse. All I know is that the agony in my mind and heart was altered by the reality of God's love. He has taken my despair and replaced it with hope. I feel liberated so that I could respond more in love and grace with people. This has filled me with great hope. I am still going through the healing process, but I know I will be fine. It all begins with a choice and supernatural help.

July 2018 Three years and three months after the crash.

I didn't bother to make playing golf again, a goal. I was convinced I could not do it with one arm. I had received many mailings from Gaylord's Adaptive Sports Program through the past three years, but I had never bothered to read them. Beth had encouraged me to give golf a try. I had nothing to lose. If I couldn't accomplish it, I wouldn't give it another thought.

It had been three years and one month since I had left Gaylord in my wheelchair. I still had so many surgeries ahead of me back in August 2015. It was now September 2018, and I was happy to have walked into Gaylord on my own power. That, itself, was a major victory. My first stop was to visit many of my old therapists and nurses. It was good to see them. It was difficult for me to see the old room, halls, and gym. I had arrived around lunchtime, and the halls had that familiar smell of institution food. The patients were all different, but the same intense injuries filled the halls. Old feelings of loneliness had returned. I fought it off, by focusing on the old friends I was visiting.

The golf tutor had a special tool to tee the ball up for me. He had encouraged me to settle down over the ball. It was difficult. My heart was racing and my right hand was squeezing the club. I had taken the club back for my first swing, and I had missed the ball entirely. That was the last miss. I had gotten in a groove from then on. I couldn't believe that I had been so successful. I was ecstatic. Playing golf with one arm was a total surprise. I felt like I was given a new gift.

Gaylord Moment- This is really the end.

Whenever I pushed the button for the nurse, someone on the other end would ask me what I wanted. I would respond, "Can someone come in here and move my tray closer?" Their response was always, "Someone will be in a minute." Minutes often turned to long periods of absence. However, when I pushed the pain button, they were in my room in an instant. I learned a valuable lesson. I only pushed the pain button. In a flash they were in. "What's wrong, Vin?"

"My arm hurts. Can someone adjust it? ...by the way, can someone move my tray closer?"

ABOUT THE AUTHOR

Vinny Carbone went to Fairfield Woods Jr. High School now Fairfield Woods Middle School where he now teaches. He is now into his thirtieth year in Fairfield. He feels fortunate to be back in the classroom after two and a half years. He is thankful to his Principal Dr. Gary Rosato for saving his teaching spot. He enjoys every day knowing that each day is a gift. He loves spending time with friends at his favorite coffee shop. Reading, team teaching Sunday school with his wife, painting, and collecting rocks or astronaut autographs take up much of his time. His friends and family are what is important to him- and Wally.

With my buddy Wally

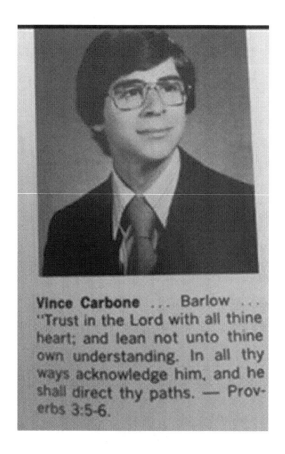

Vince Carbone ... Barlow ...
"Trust in the Lord with all thine
heart; and lean not unto thine
own understanding. In all thy
ways acknowledge him, and he
shall direct thy paths. — Proverbs 3:5-6.

Footnotes

1 Chuck Hadad, "Why some 13-year-olds check social media 100 times a day," CNN, October 13, 2015.
https://www.cnn.com/2015/10/05/health/being-13-teens-social-media-study/index.html

2 Ibid.
https://www.cnn.com/2015/10/05/health/being-13-teens-social-media-study/index.html

3 Neal Boudette, "Biggest Spike in Traffic Deaths in 50 Years? Blame Apps", New York Times, November 15, 2016.
https://www.nytimes.com/2016/11/16/business/tech-distractions-blamed-for-rise-in-traffic-fatalities.html

[4] Sylane Mack, *Convinced!*, CreateSpace, 2009. page 117.

[5] Ibid, page 120.

[6] Ibid, page 121.

[7] Ann Spanger and Lois Tverberg, *Sitting at the Feet of Rabbi Jesus*, 2009, Grand Rapids, MI, Zondervan. page 37.

[8] Ibid, page 37.

[9] Ann Spanger and Lois Tverberg, *Sitting at the Feet of Rabbi Jesus*, 2009, Grand Rapids, MI, Zondervan. page 39

[10] Lois Tverberg, *Walking in the Dust of Rabbi Jesus*, 2012, Grand Rapids, MI, Zondervan, page 161.

[11] Ibid, page 133.

Bibliography

Boudette, Neal E. "Biggest Spike in Traffic Deaths in 50 Years? Blame Apps," New York
Times, November 15, 2016.

Hadad, Chuck. "Why some 13-year-olds check social media 100 times a day," CNN, October 13, 2013.

Holy Bible, New International Version. 1984, Grand Rapids, Mich.: Zondervan.

Mack, Sylane. *Convinced!* CreateSpace, USA, 2009.

Spangler, Ann; Tverberg, Lois. *Sitting at the Feet of Rabbi Jesus, How the Jewishness of Jesus can Transform Your Faith*. Grand Rapids: Zondervan, 2009.

Tverberg, Lois. *Walking in the Dust of Rabbi Jesus, How The Jewish Words of Jesus Can Change Your Life*. Grand Rapids: Zondervan, 2012.

49745672R00064

Made in the USA
Middletown, DE
21 June 2019